JOSEPH HAYDN

MISSA IN ANGUSTIIS

für SATB soli, Chor und Orchester
for SATB Soli, Choir and Orchestra

Hob. XXII:11

Nelson-Messe / Nelson Mass

Herausgegeben von / Edited by

Klaus Burmeister

Klavierauszug von / Vocal Score by

Wilhelm Weismann

ALLE RECHTE VORBEHALTEN · ALL RIGHTS RESERVED

EDITION PETERS

LEIPZIG · LONDON · NEW YORK

Inhalt / Contents

I. KYRIE 1
Soprano solo e Coro

II. GLORIA

Gloria in excelsis Deo 16
Soli e Coro

Qui tollis 26
Soprano solo, Basso solo e Coro

Quoniam tu solus 32
Soli e Coro

III. CREDO

Credo in unum Deum 42
Coro

Et incarnatus 48
Soli e Coro

Et resurrexit 53
Soprano solo e Coro

IV. SANCTUS 64
Coro

V. BENEDICTUS 70
Soli e Coro

VI. AGNUS DEI

Agnus Dei 82
Soli

Dona nobis 85
Coro

Nachwort / Afterword 95

BESETZUNG / ORCHESTRATION*)
Flauto – 2 Oboi – 2 Clarinetti – Fagotto
2 Corni – 3 Trombe – Timpani – Organo
Violino I – Violino II – Viola – Violoncello – Contrabbasso
Soli: Soprano – Alto – Tenore – Basso
Coro

*) *zur Besetzung vgl. Nachwort / for Orchestration cf. Afterword*

Aufführungsdauer / Duration: ca. 40 Min.

Missa in Angustiis
("Nelson-Messe")
I. KYRIE

Joseph Haydn (1732-1809)
Hob. XXII:11
Herausgegeben von Klaus Burmeister
Klavierauszug von Wilhelm Weismann

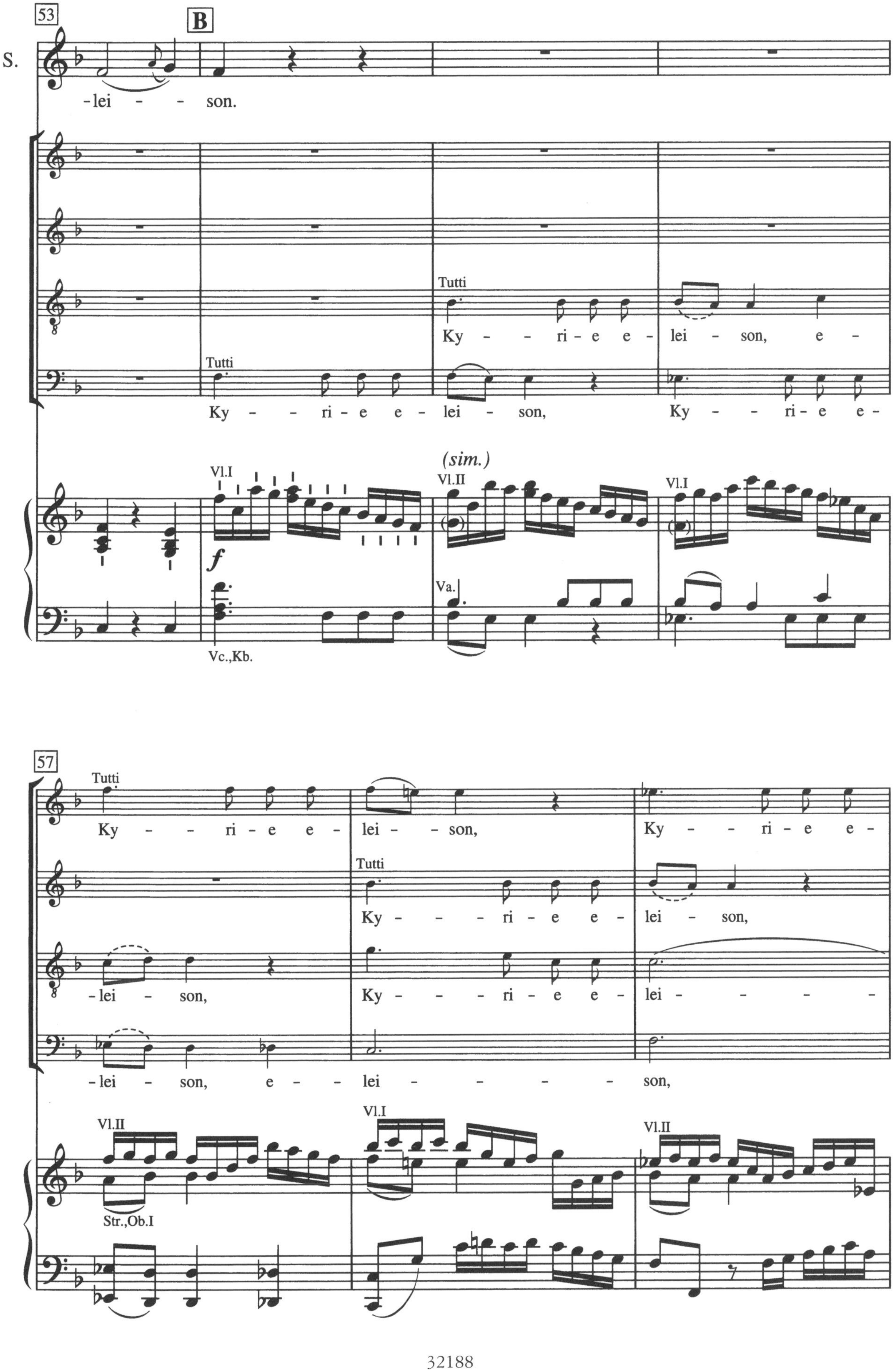
53
B
S.
-lei - - son.
Tutti
Ky - - ri - e e - lei - son, e -
Tutti
Ky - - ri - e e - lei - son, Ky - - ri - e e -
(sim.)
Vl.I
Vl.II
Vl.I
f
Va.
Vc.,Kb.
57
Tutti
Ky - - ri - e e - lei - - son, Ky - - ri - e e -
Tutti
Ky - - - ri - e e - lei - son,
-lei - son, Ky - - ri - e e - lei - - - -
-lei - son, e - - lei - - - - son,
Vl.II
Str.,Ob.I
Vl.I
Vl.II

9

II. GLORIA

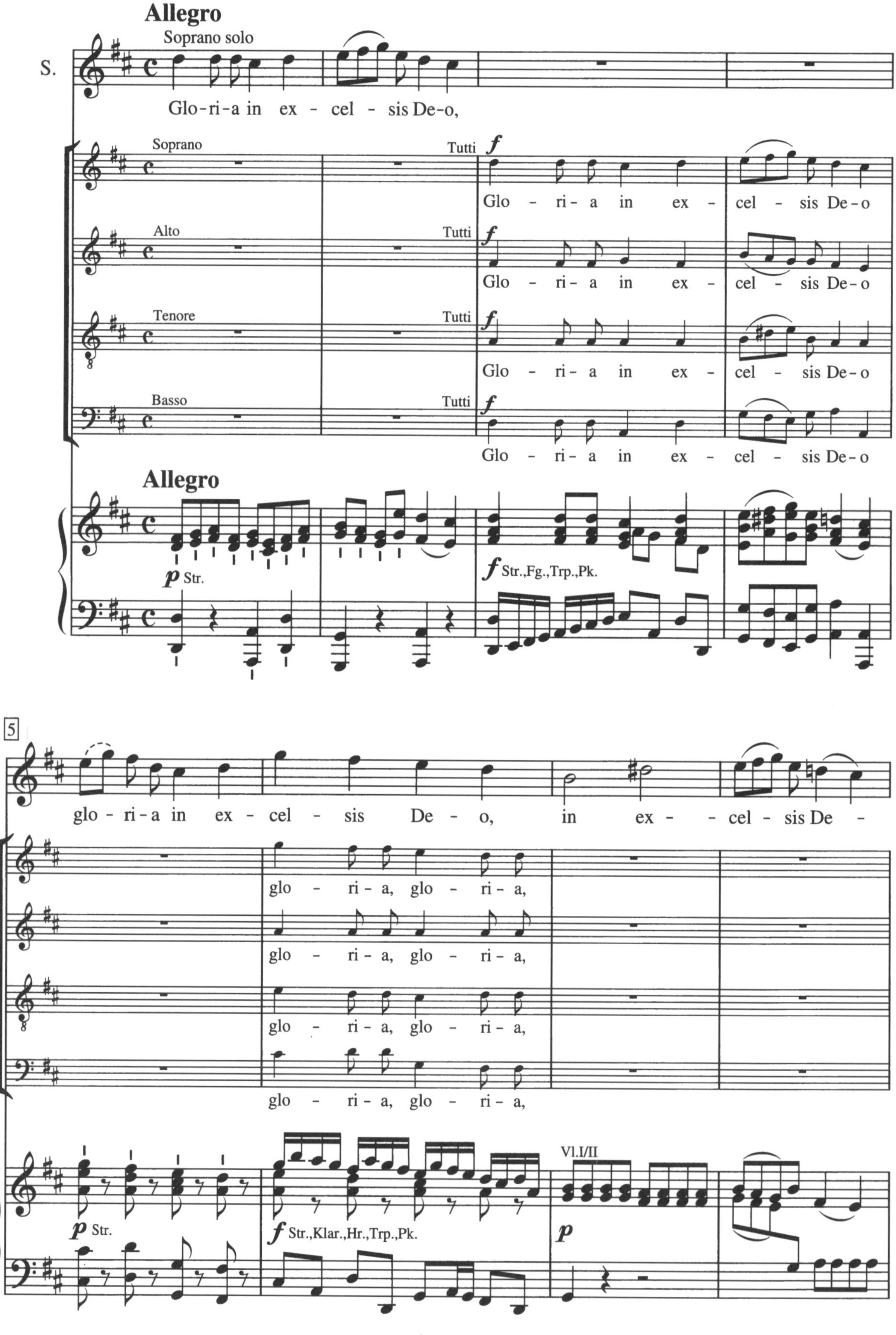
Allegro
Soprano solo
S.
Glo-ri-a in ex - cel - sis De-o,
Soprano
Alto
Tenore
Basso
Tutti
Glo - ri- a in ex - cel - sis De-o
Allegro
Str.
Str.,Fg.,Trp.,Pk.
5
glo - ri-a in ex - cel - sis De - o, in ex - - cel - sis De -
glo - ri- a, glo - ri- a,
Str.
Str.,Klar.,Hr.,Trp.,Pk.
Vl.I/II

Qui tollis

Quoniam tu solus

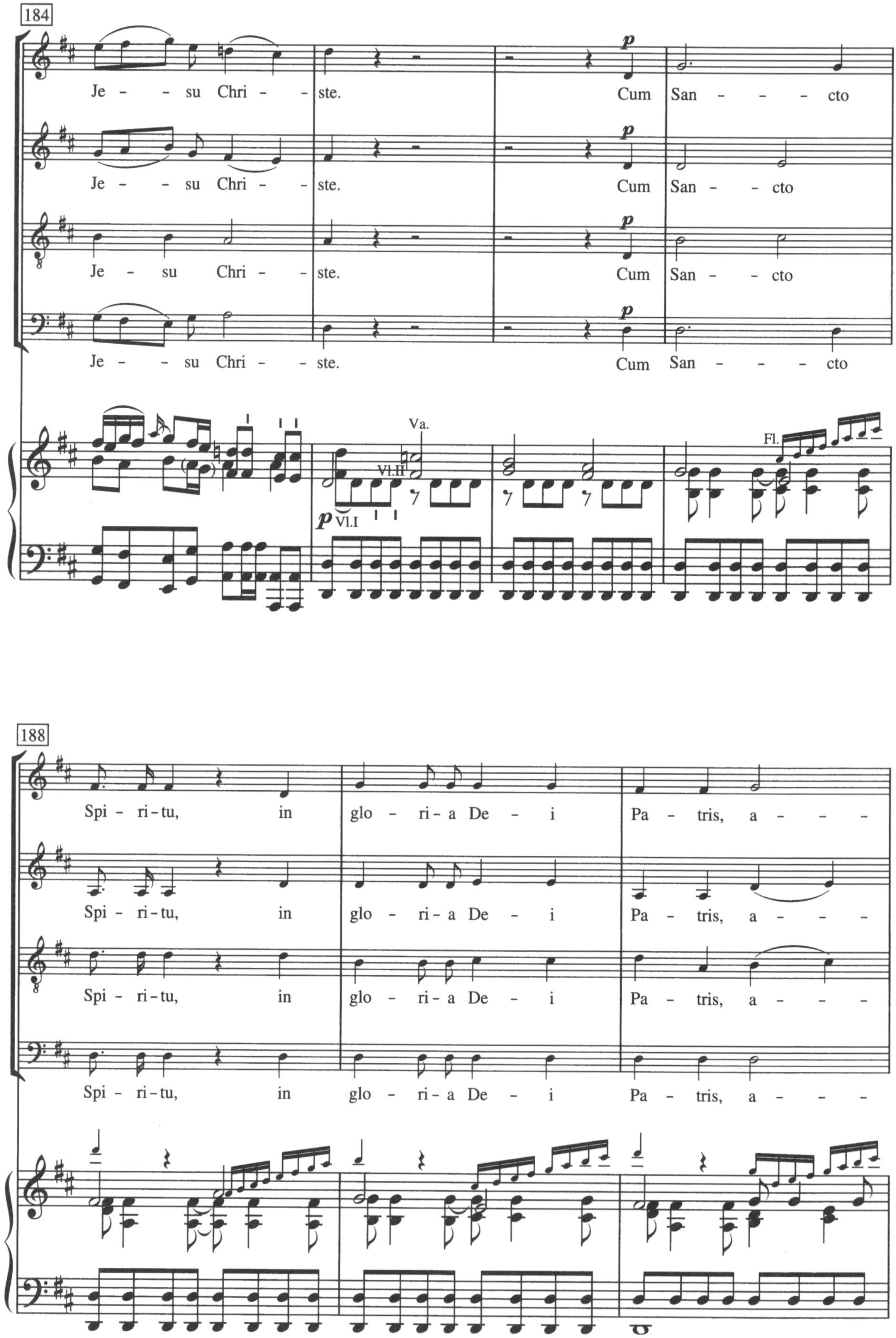
184
Je - su Chri - ste. Cum San - cto
Je - su Chri - ste. Cum San - cto
Je - su Chri - ste. Cum San - cto
Je - su Chri - ste. Cum San - cto
Va.
Vl.II
p Vl.I
Fl.
188
Spi - ri-tu, in glo - ri-a De - i Pa - tris, a -
Spi - ri-tu, in glo - ri-a De - i Pa - tris, a -
Spi - ri-tu, in glo - ri-a De - i Pa - tris, a -
Spi - ri-tu, in glo - ri-a De - i Pa - tris, a -

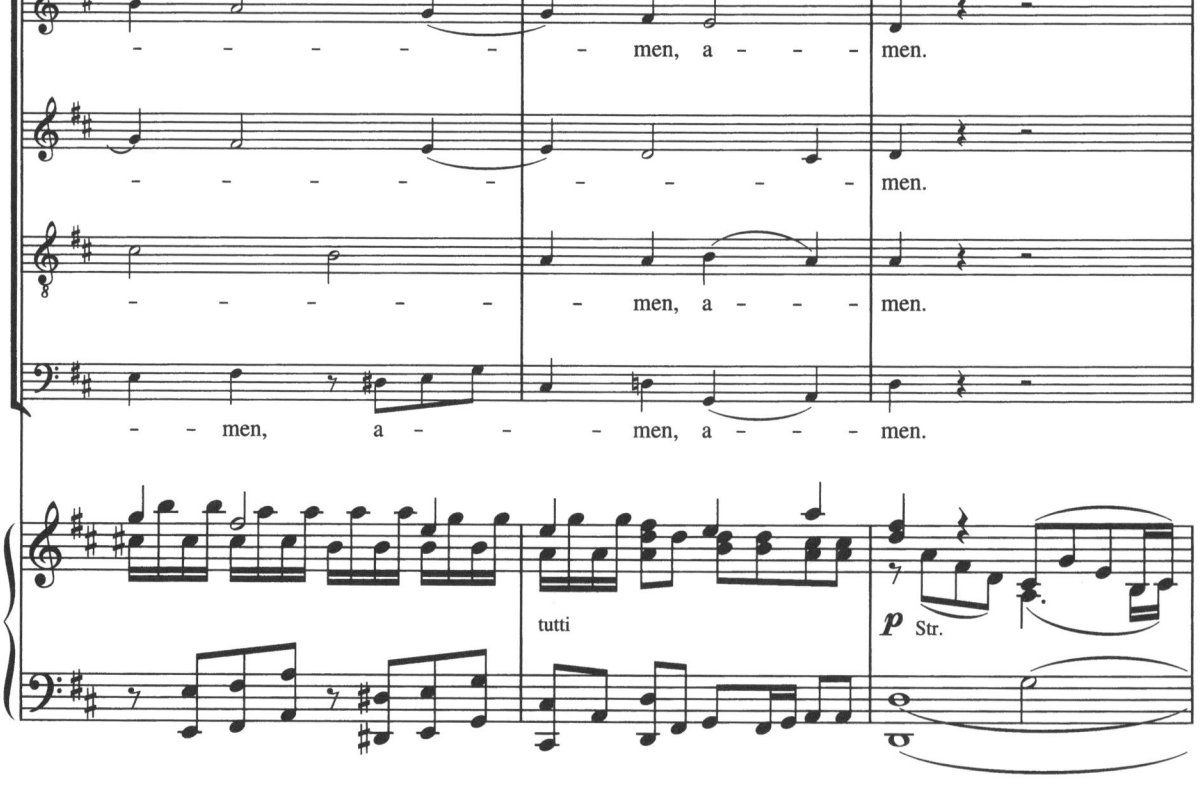

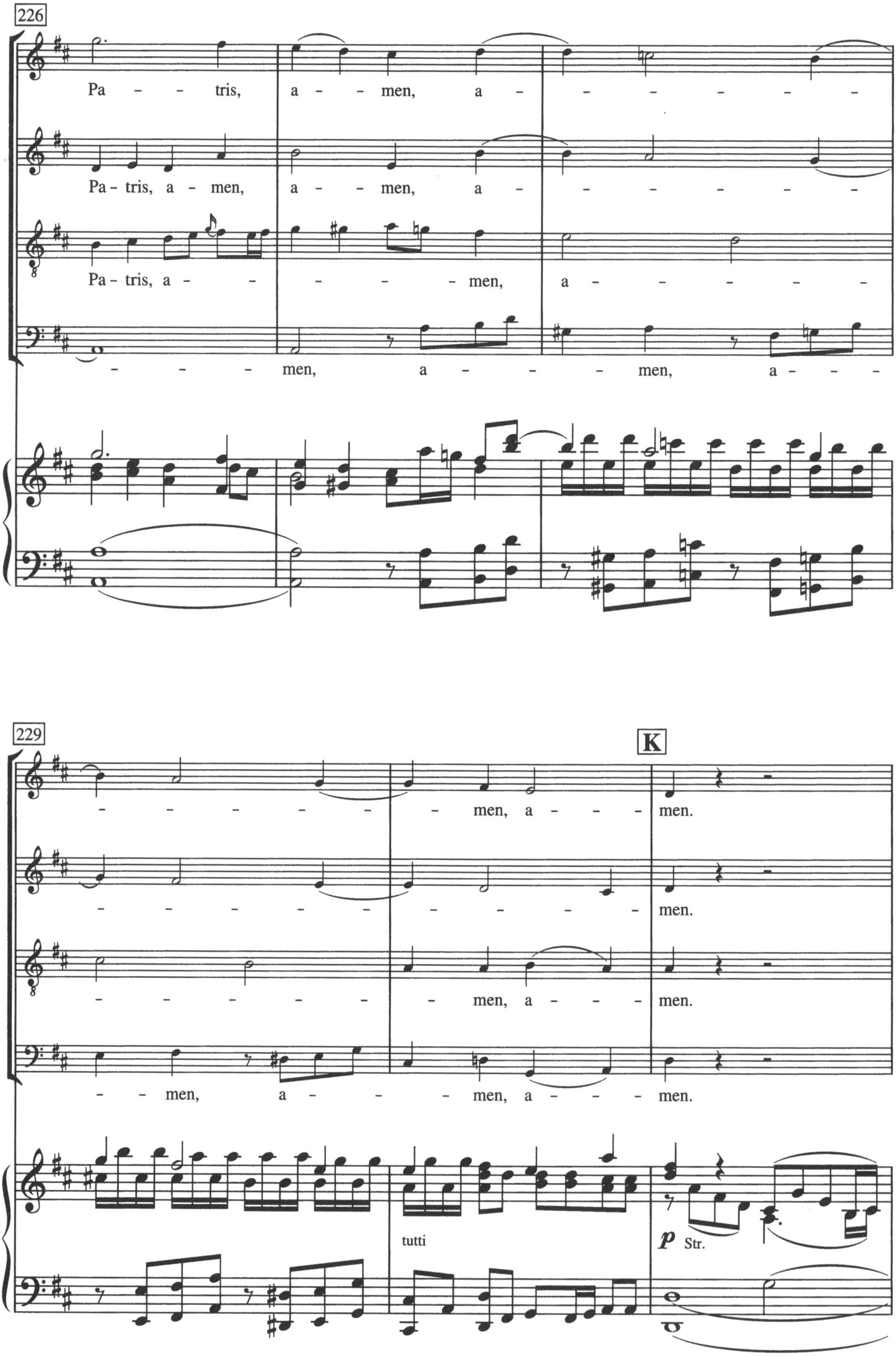
226
Pa - - tris, a - - men, a - - - - - - -
Pa-tris, a - men, a - - men, a - - - - - - - -
Pa-tris, a - - - - - men, a - - - - - - -
- - - - men, a - - - - men, a - - -
229
K
- - - - - - - men, a - - - - men.
- - - - - - - - - - - - men.
- - - - - - - men, a - - - - men.
- - men, a - - - - men, a - - - - men.
tutti
p Str.

III. CREDO

-tum ante omnia saecula.
na-tum ante omnia sae-cu-la.
-tum ante omnia saecula.
na-tum ante omnia sae-cu-

De-um de De-o, lu-men de lu-mi-ne, De-um
-la. De-um de De-o, lu-men de lu-mi-ne,
De-um de De-o, lu-men de lu-mi-ne, De-um
-la. De-um de De-o, lu-men de lu-mi-ne,

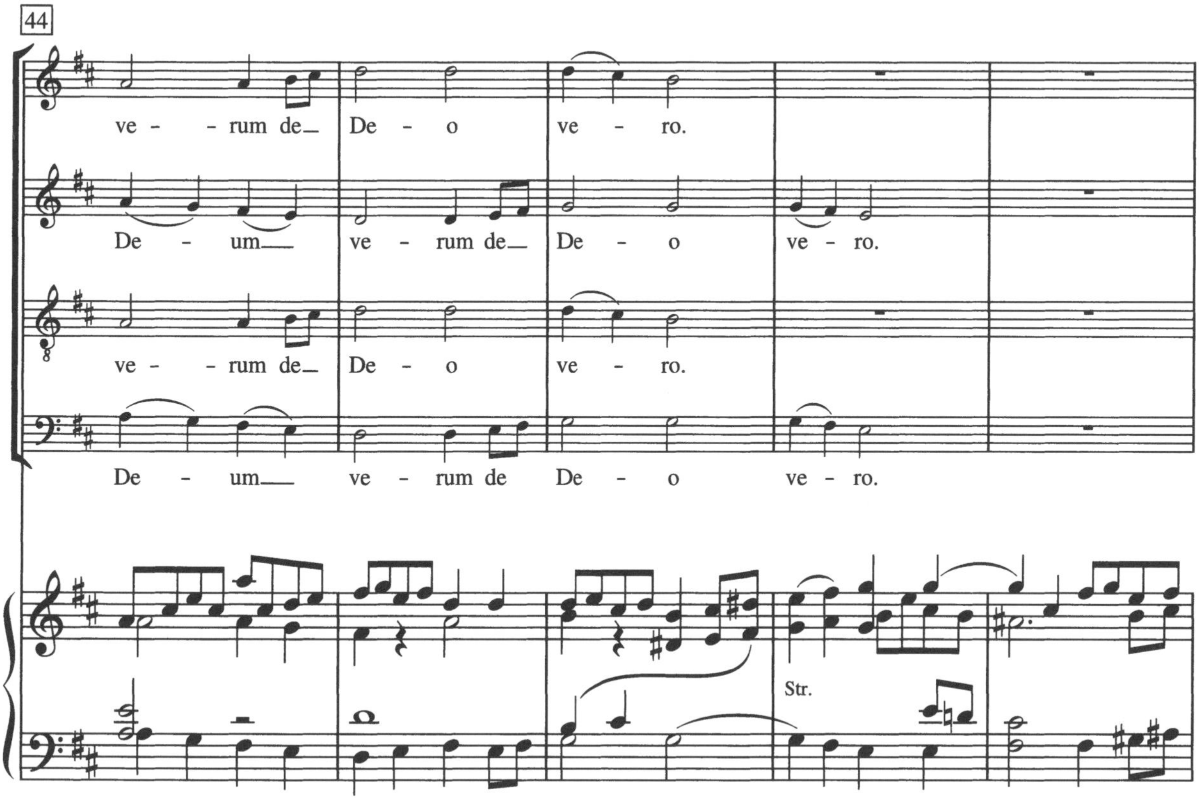
44
ve - - rum de Deo ve - ro.
De - um ve - rum de De - o ve - ro.
ve - - rum de De - o ve - ro.
De - um ve - rum de De - o ve - ro.
Str.

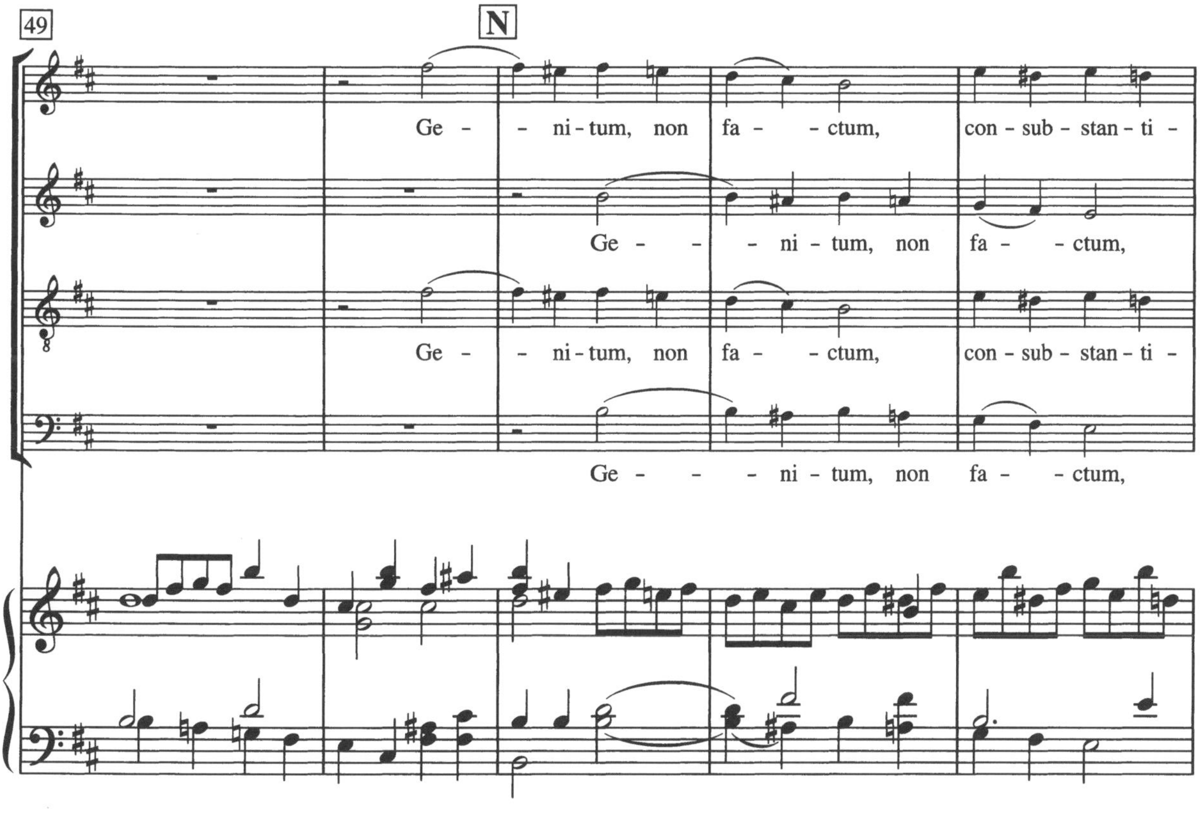
49
N
Ge - - ni - tum, non fa - - ctum, con - sub - stan - ti -
Ge - - - ni - tum, non fa - - ctum,
Ge - - ni - tum, non fa - - ctum, con - sub - stan - ti -
Ge - - - ni - tum, non fa - - ctum,

Et incarnatus

Et resurrexit

IV. SANCTUS

V. BENEDICTUS

VI. AGNUS DEI

Dona nobis

112
-cem, do — — na
-cem, do — — na
-cem, do — — na
-cem, do — — na

114
no — — bis pa — — cem, pa — — cem, pa — cem.
no — — bis pa — — cem, pa — — cem, pa — cem.
no — — bis pa — — cem, pa — — cem, pa — cem.
no — — bis pa — — cem, pa — — cem, pa — cem.

Nachwort

Joseph Haydn hat während der gesamten Zeit seines künstlerischen Schaffens kirchliche Werke komponiert, oftmals für einen bestimmten Anlaß, den es zu bedenken galt. Allein 14 Meßkompositionen sind darunter, die nachweislich ihrem Schöpfer zuzuordnen sind, auch wenn eine davon, die als seine zweite gilt, nicht erhalten ist.[1] Nach der sogenannten *Marienzeller Messe* (Hob XXII: 8), komponiert 1782, trat eine längere Pause von 14 Jahren ein, bevor Haydn seine nächsten Messen schrieb. Es sollten zwischen 1796 und 1802 die sechs großen Hochämter[2] werden und – darüber hinaus – *Die sieben letzten Worte unseres Erlösers am Kreuze* (in der Vokalfassung, beendet spätestens Anfang 1796), die Oratorien *Die Schöpfung* (1796-98) und *Die Jahreszeiten* (fertiggestellt 1801), die nachgerade dem schon vorhandenen Ruhm des Meisters eine neue Dimension hinzufügten und für ihn selbst von höchster Bedeutung in seinem Schaffen wurden. Haydn war, nachdem er seinen zweiten Englandaufenthalt (am 15. August 1795 begann seine Rückreise) beendet hatte, ausdrücklich von seinem neuen Fürsten, Nicolaus II.[3], beauftragt worden, jährlich eine Messe zu komponieren. Sie alle sollten für die Namensfeste[4] der Gattin seines Dienstherrn, der Fürstin Maria Josepha Hermenegild Esterházy, gedacht sein. Wenn auch seitens der Forschung eine gewisse Unsicherheit besteht, ob wirklich alle diese Messen zum Namenstag der Fürstin aufgeführt, d.h. uraufgeführt wurden, so ist dies für das dritte Werk, die d-Moll-Messe, genannt *Nelsonmesse*, mit einiger Sicherheit feststellbar. Haydn selbst hat die Entstehungszeit seiner Partitur im Autograph genau datiert (1. Notenseite: *„798. 10ten Julj Eisenstadt."*, letzte Notenseite: *„Fine Laus Deo. 31. August:"*). Sie wurde also rechtzeitig fertig, um eiligst die Stimmen kopieren und das Werk proben zu können. Doch die Aufführung fand dann offensichtlich nicht – wie früher angenommen – am 9. September, einem Sonntag (Fest Maria Namen), statt, sondern aus unbekannten Gründen erst am 23. September, wie ein Zeitzeuge seinem Tagebuch anvertraute.[5]

Über die Herkunft des Beinamens *Nelsonmesse* gibt es allerlei Vermutungen, wenn auch keine darauf hindeutet, daß Haydn diesen Begriff selbst geprägt hat. Angeblich soll Haydn berichtet haben, daß er während der Komposition des *Benedictus* vom Sieg Nelsons über die Franzosen[6] erfahren und *„das Bild eines blasenden Kouriers durchaus nicht aus seiner Phantasie verdrängen"* habe können, *„und da die Idee seines Benedictus mit jener so verwandt gewesen, so habe er die obligate Trompete"* – drei Trompeten unisono – *„dazu gesetzt"*.[7] Die Glaubwürdigkeit dieser Quelle ist insofern anzuzweifeln, als die Nachricht vom Sieg Nelsons erst Wochen später, Mitte September, in Wien eingetroffen ist.[8] Eine entsprechende Eintragung in Haydns Nachlaßverzeichnis aus dem Jahre 1809 beweist aber immerhin, daß die Messe ihren Beinamen bereits zu seinen Lebzeiten erhalten haben muß. Obwohl der Komponist selbst das Werk in seinem (größtenteils) eigenhändig verfaßten *Entwurf-Katalog*[9] *„Missa in Angustijs"* („Messe in Bedrängnis, Not und Gefahr") benannte[10] – im Autograph hat er es lediglich als *„Missa"* bezeichnet –, so scheint doch seine Zustimmung zu dieser Benennung nicht ganz abwegig zu sein. Einerseits hat im Jahre 1800 eine Begegnung zwischen Nelson (mit Lady Hamilton) und Haydn stattgefunden, wie z.B. Georg August Griesinger, der als Beauftragter des Leipziger Verlagshauses Breitkopf & Härtel seit 1799 mit Haydn in Verbindung stand, berichtete[11], andererseits ist ein Plan der Seeschlacht bei Abukir im Nachlaß Haydns gefunden worden, was auf ein spezielles Interesse des Komponisten schließen läßt. Das *Elßler'sche Haydn-Verzeichnis*[12] von 1805 enthält allerdings keinen authentischen Hinweis auf Nelson. Erst zu einem offensichtlich späteren Zeitpunkt hat eine fremde Hand dort den Beinamen *„Nelson-Missa"* hinzugefügt. Der Erstdruck von Breitkopf & Härtel aus dem Jahre 1803 erschien ebenfalls ohne jeden Beinamen. Dort wird das Werk schlicht als *„Messe à 4 Voix* (mit Aufzählung der Instrumente) ... *N° III."* bezeichnet.

Haydn instrumentierte die *Nelsonmesse* nicht in einer größeren Bläserbesetzung, wie er es früher gelegentlich, später immer getan hat, sondern lediglich mit drei Trompeten, mit Pauken, Streichern und einer obligaten Orgel.[13] Griesinger benennt den Grund in einem Brief vom 4. Dezember 1802[14] an Breitkopf & Härtel, die sich um die Erwerbung der Druckrechte bemühten: *„Haydn sagte mir, er habe in der Messe ... die Blasinstrumente auf die Orgel gesezt, weil damals der Fürst Esterhazy die Spieler der blasenden Instrum. verabschiedet hatte. Er rathe Ihnen aber, alles was in der Orgelstimme als obligat vorkommt, auf die Blasinstrumente überzutragen und so druken zu lassen."* Es handelte sich also um einen Notbehelf, der behoben werden sollte. Inzwischen – seit dem Jahre 1800 – war die Kapelle aber wieder vollständig mit allen dort üblichen Blasinstrumenten besetzt, wie Griesinger seinem Leipziger Auftraggeber mitteilte.[15] So enthalten verschiedene Orchestermateriale aus dieser Zeit Ergänzungsstimmen für zusätzliche Holzbläser, wenige aber 2 Hörner; alle behalten den vollständigen Orgelpart bei. Es war nicht auszumachen, welche Materiale außer einer Partiturabschrift für die Druckausgabe vorlagen. Die Blasinstrumentenpartien im Erstdruck ähneln in vielen Details dem Eisenstädter Material[16], selbst dort, wo die Orgel in Haydns Partiturautograph nicht eigens ausgeschrieben, d.h. nicht obligat besetzt ist. Sie zeigen aber darüber hinaus deutliche Spuren bewußter Eingriffe bzw. Veränderungen einer kenntnisreichen Hand, möglicherweise die des nachmaligen Thomaskantors August Eberhard Müller. Allerdings fehlen im Erstdruck die Klarinetten und Hörner gänzlich, die übrigen Holzbläser hingegen sind sogar in allen Teilen der Messe besetzt. Der obligate Orgelpart ist – eingedenk der Mitteilung Griesingers, die Blasinstrumente an dessen Stelle zu setzen – im Erstdruck nicht enthalten; die Orgel übernimmt aber in der üblichen Weise das Generalbaßspiel.[17]

Für eine quellenkritische Neuausgabe dieser Messe ist die Entscheidung nicht ganz einfach, welcher Bläserbesetzung der Vorrang einzuräumen ist. Sie alle sind, ob mit oder ohne Klarinetten, mit oder ohne Hörner[18], nicht von Haydn. Bereits der Herausgeber der Gesamtausgabe[19], Günter Thomas, hat der Eisenstädter Fassung den Vorrang eingeräumt mit Rücksicht auf die größte Nähe zum Komponisten, auch wenn nirgends belegt ist, daß Haydn jemals diese Bläserfassung für eine Aufführung benutzt hat. Haydns eigenhändige Korrekturspuren sind lediglich in einigen ursprünglichen Stimmen (erste Schicht) des Esterházy-Materials festzustellen, so in einem der „authentischen" Exemplare von Violine I und II, die Johann Elßler, persönlicher Diener und Kopist Haydns, abgeschrieben hat. Allerdings kannte Haydn auch die Leipziger Bläserfassung des Erstdrucks, denn zwei Exemplare haben sich in seinem Nachlaß befunden. Wenn auch in der jetzigen Neuausgabe wieder der Eisenstädter Bläserbesetzung Vorrang eingeräumt wurde, so deshalb, weil möglicherweise Intentionen des Komponisten dahinterstehen, auf alle Fälle aber den Eisenstädter Aufführungs- und Besetzungsgewohnheiten entsprochen werden soll.

Der vorgelegte Klavierauszug basiert einerseits auf der neuen quellenkritischen Partiturausgabe (EP 8989), andererseits auf Wilhelm Weismanns Klavierpart der *Nelsonmesse* aus dem Jahre 1932 (EP 4351). Weismann benutzte seinerzeit den Breitkopfschen Erstdruck als einzige Quelle für seine Partiturausgabe (EP 4342). So wurde es jetzt nicht nur erforderlich, für unsere Neuausgabe den vorhandenen Klaviersatz zu revidieren, sondern vor allem die Vokalstimmen restlos mit dem Autograph abzustimmen, ganz im Sinne der neuen Partiturausgabe. Der Vokalpart hält sich somit eng an das Partiturautograph, wird lediglich dort ohne Kennzeichnung aus den authentischen Stimmen ergänzt, wo sich musikalische Selbstverständlichkeiten erkennen lassen (dynamische Angaben, Bögen). Die wenigen Ergänzungen des Herausgebers – begründet in Analogien – sind durch Klammern bzw. gestrichelte Bögen gekennzeichnet. Über Einzelheiten von quellenkritischen Entscheidungen gibt eine tabellarische Übersicht der Lesarten in der Partitur Auskunft. Im *Credo* ist der liturgisch gewichtige Satz „*Et in unum Dominum Jesum Christum, Filium Dei unigenitum*" nicht vertont worden, auch fehlen die Worte „*qui ex Patre Filioque procedit*".

Klaus Burmeister

---

[1] Zahlreiche weitere Messen kursieren unter Haydns Namen, doch scheint sich die Forschung längst darüber einig, diese Werke anderen Komponisten zuordnen zu müssen (siehe Hob. XXII: C1-B13).

[2] Es waren dies die *Paukenmesse* (Hob. XXII: 9), die *Heiligmesse* (Nr. 10), die *Nelsonmesse* (Nr. 11), die *Theresienmesse* (Nr. 12), die *Schöpfungsmesse* (Nr. 13) und die *Harmoniemesse* (Nr. 14).

[3] Haydns ehemaliger Dienstherr, Fürst Nicolaus „der Prächtige" war 1790 gestorben. Dessen Nachfolger, Anton, löste die Esterházysche Kapelle (bis auf die Bläser für die Jagd) unmittelbar danach auf. Nach Antons Tod (22.1.1795) jedoch rief dessen Nachfolger, Nicolaus II., die Kapelle wieder zusammen und übertrug Haydn nominell die Leitung mit der (einzigen) Aufgabe, jährlich eine Messe zu komponieren. In einem Brief vom 10.11.1799 an den „*Musikdirektor Cornelius Knoblich im Kloster Grissau*" dokumentiert Haydn einen solchen Auftrag. Er habe in seinen „*alten Tagen aus billiger anordnung meines dermahligen Jungen Fürsten seit 4 Jahren, alljährlich eine neue Mess zu Componiren*" (Dénes Bartha [Hg.], *Joseph Haydn – Gesammelte Briefe und Aufzeichnungen*, Kassel u.a. 1965, S. 331).

[4] Es war Regel, die Zelebration des Namenstages der Fürstin (8. September) auf den jeweils folgenden Sonntag (Fest Maria Namen) zu legen.

[5] Peter Rosenbaum schreibt: „*Sonntag, den 23ten: ... Um 10 Uhr gieng ich ... in die große Kirche, wo das neue Amt von Haydn gemacht wurde ...*" (zit. nach Carl Maria Brand, *Die Messen von Joseph Haydn*, Würzburg 1941, S. 311)

[6] Seeschlacht bei Abukir zwischen 1. und 3. August 1798, in der Admiral Nelson die französische Flotte vernichtend schlug

[7] *Ueber Musik und Schauspielkunst in Wien*, in: *Journal des Luxus und der Moden*, 15. Band, Weimar 1800, S. 330f. Der unbekannte Autor erlebte 1800 eine Aufführung der Messe in der Wiener Schottenkirche und berichetet über sein Gespräch mit Haydn.

[8] Edward Olleson, *Haydn in the Diaries of Count Karl von Zinsendorf*, in: Das Haydn Jahrbuch, Bd. II, Wien 1963/64, S. 54

[9] Jens Peter Larsen (Hg.), *Drei Haydn-Kataloge in Faksimile mit Einleitung und ergänzenden Themenverzeichnissen*, Kopenhagen 1941

[10] Ebd., S. 17

[11] „*Wien, d. 21. Jan. 1801 ... An Milady Hamilton fand Hn. einen großen Verehrer. Sie machte einen Besuch mit Nelson auf Esterhazys Gütern in Ungarn ...*"; Günter Thomas (Hg.), *Griesingers Briefe über Haydn*, in: Haydn-Studien, Bd. I, 2. Heft, München-Duisburg 1966, S. 66

[12] Siehe Anmerkung 9

[13] Die autographe Partitur benennt auf der 1. Notenseite folgendes Instrumentarium: 2 Clarini [im 1. Kyrie-Takt steht jedoch die Anweisung „*a tre*"] / Tympano / Violino 1mo / 2do / Viola / Alto / [folgen Gesangstimmen] Organo [notiert auf zwei Systemen].

[14] Günter Thomas (Hg.), *Griesingers Briefe über Haydn*, a.a.O., S. 91

[15] Brief vom 15.11.1800, a.a.O, S. 66: „*Fürst Esterhazy hat seine Capelle mit 8 Gliedern vermehrt, so daß jetzt wieder eine vollständige Harmonie beysammen ist.*"

[16] Die Stimmenabschrift aus dem Esterházy-Archiv ist auf einem Umschlag betitelt mit: „*Anno 1798. / Missa in D. / a / 4. Vocce. Conc^{to}. / 2. Violini. / Viola. / Flauto. / 2. Oboi. / 2. Clarinetti / Fagotto. / 2. Corni. / 3. Clarini. / Tympano / Violoncello è Basso. / con. / Organo. / Del Sig^{re} Gius: Haydn.*"; von fremder Hand ist der Beiname *Nelson* nachgetragen.

[17] Der vollständige Titel des Partitur-Erstdruckes von Breitkopf & Härtel lautet: Messe à 4 Voix avec accompagnement de 2 Violons, Viola et Basse, une Flûte, 2 Hautbois, 2 Bassons, 2 Cors, 3 Trompettes, Timbales et Orgue ... No III. Merkwürdigerweise sind zwar die Hörner benannt, aber im Partiturdruck nicht enthalten.

[18] Stimmensätze, die einen gewissen Anspruch auf Authentizität haben – zumindest weil einige Kopien aus der ersten Schicht Johann Elßler zugeordnet werden können –, sind aus Klosterneuburg, Prag (Bestand des Lobkowitz-Archivs) und Wien (Archiv der Hofmusikkapelle) bekannt, enthalten jedoch allesamt keine Klarinetten und Hörner, in Wien, wegen der örtlichen Aufführungspraxis, jedoch zwei zusätzliche Trombonen.

[19] Joseph Haydn Werke, Reihe XXIII, Bd. 3 *Messen Nr. 9-10*, München-Duisburg, 1971

Afterword

Joseph Haydn composed church music throughout his entire career, often for particular occasions that called for special celebration. No fewer than fourteen Mass settings are known to have proceeded from his pen, although one of them, thought to be his second, is no longer extant today.[1] The so-called "Mariazell" Mass of 1782 (Hob. XXII: 8) was followed by a lengthy hiatus of fourteen years before Haydn wrote his next Mass. The years from 1796 to 1802 witnessed the creation of his six great settings of the High Mass[2] as well as the vocal version of *The Seven Last Words of Our Savior on the Cross* (finished by early 1796 at the latest), *The Creation* (1796-8), and *The Seasons* (finished in 1801). These works added a new dimension to the composer's already towering reputation and were considered by Haydn himself to be among the most significant in his œuvre. Having returned from his second stay in England (the return journey began on 15 August 1795), Haydn was specifically enjoined by his new employer, Prince Nicolaus II[3], to produce a new Mass setting each year to celebrate the name day[4] of his consort, Princess Maria Josepha Hermenegild Esterházy. Although scholars are not entirely certain whether all of these Masses were actually given their first performances on the princess's name day, we can be reasonably sure that this was the case with the third work, the so-called "Nelson" Mass in D minor. Haydn himself precisely noted the dates of the work's genesis in his score, adding "10 July 1798 Eisenstadt" on the first page of music and "Fine Laus Deo 31 August" on the final page. In short, it was completed in good time for the instrumental parts to be written out and the work to go into rehearsal. None the less, the performance apparently did not, as was once assumed, take place on Sunday, 9 September (the Feast of the Most Holy Name of Mary). Instead, as a contemporary observer confided to his diary[5], it was postponed for unknown reasons to the 23rd of September.

There have been many conjectures as to the origins of the work's nickname. None of them, however, suggest that it was coined by Haydn. The composer is said to have remarked that while composing the *Benedictus* he learned of Nelson's victory over the French[6] and "could not suppress the image of a trumpeting herald from his mind ... and as the idea of his *Benedictus* was so closely related to that image he added the obligato trumpets" – i.e. three trumpets playing in unison.[7] The credibility of this source must be questioned as the news of the victory only arrived in Vienna weeks later, in mid-September.[8] Be that as it may, an entry of 1809 in the inventory of Haydn's posthumous estate reveals that the Mass must have received its nickname during the composer's lifetime. Haydn himself, in the largely autograph catalogue of his works (*Entwurf-Katalog*[9]), referred to it as the *Missa in Angustijs* (the "Mass in Adversity")[10] and his autograph manuscript merely gives it the title of "Missa". None the less, it is entirely conceivable that the nickname met with his approval. He met Nelson (with Lady Hamilton) personally in 1800, as we know from Georg August Griesinger, who maintained contacts with Haydn from 1799 as a commercial agent for the Leipzig publishers Breitkopf & Härtel.[11] Moreover, a map of the Battle of the Nile was found in Haydn's estate, which suggests that the composer took a special interest in it. However, the "Elssler Catalogue" of 1805[12] does not contain an authorial reference to Nelson as the nickname "Nelson-Missa" was apparently added in a different hand at a later date. Nor did Breitkopf & Härtel's first edition of 1803 appear with a nickname, the work being merely referred to as *Messe à 4 Voix* (followed by a list of instruments) *N° III*.

Rather than scoring the "Nelson" Mass for a large wind band, as he sometimes did in his early pieces and always in his later ones, Haydn merely set it for three trumpets, timpani, strings, and obligato organ.[13] The reason for this is recounted by Griesinger in a letter of 4 December 1802[14] to Breitkopf & Härtel, who were engaged in obtaining the publication rights: "Haydn told me that in his Mass... he had transferred the wind instruments to the organ part because the then Prince Esterházy had dismissed the wind players. He therefore advises you to transcribe to the wind instruments everything that appears obligato in the organ part and to publish [the work] in that form." In short, we are dealing here with a temporary makeshift that Haydn wished to have remedied. Since then (i.e. the year 1800), as Griesinger reported to his Leipzig employer, the Esterházy orchestra had been restored to its full size with the usual contingent of winds.[15] Accordingly, various sets of orchestral material dating from this period contain added parts for the woodwind, and a few call for two horns, whereas all retain the complete organ part. It was not possible to determine which materials, apart from a full score in the hand of a copyist, were available for the printed edition. The wind parts in the first edition resemble the Eisenstadt material[16] in many respects, even in those passages where the organ part is not separately written out (i.e. not obligato) in Haydn's autograph score. However, they also reveal clear evidence of deliberate interventions and alterations by a knowledgeable hand, perhaps August Eberhard Müller, the subsequent cantor at St Thomas's in Leipzig. In contrast, the first print lacks the clarinets and horns altogether, whereas the other woodwind instruments even appear in every section of the Mass. Nonetheless, in keeping with Griesinger's instruction to substitute winds for the obligato organ part, the first edition omits this organ part while retaining the thoroughbass figures, as was customary at the time.[17]

For the purposes of a scholarly-critical edition of the "Nelson" Mass it is no easy matter to decide which of these wind scorings should take precedence. None of them, whether or not with clarinets or horns[18], is by Haydn. The editor of the *Gesamtausgabe*, Günter Thomas[19], gave preference to the Eisenstadt version as being closest to the composer, even though there is no indication that Haydn ever used this wind version in performance. Haydn's autograph corrections are only detectable in a few original parts (first layer) of the Esterházy material; they can, for example, be found in the "authentic" copies of violins 1 and 2 written out by Johann Elssler, Haydn's personal servant and copyist. All the same, Haydn was aware of the Leipzig wind version presented in the first edition, for two copies of it were found in his posthumous estate. If we have again chosen to give precedence to the Eisenstadt wind scoring in our new edition, the reason is that it may well represent the composer's intentions, and it most certainly reflects the usages of instrumental scoring and performance in Eisenstadt.

Our vocal score is based on the new scholarly-critical edition in full score (EP 8989) and on Wilhelm Weismann's piano part of 1932 for the "Nelson" Mass (EP 4351). Weismann's sole source for his edition in score (EP 4342) was the original Breitkopf print. It therefore proved necessary, for our new edition, not only to revise the existing piano part but also, and especially, to co-ordinate the vocal parts with the autograph and bring them fully into line with the new score edition. The vocal parts therefore closely adhere to the autograph score, with unmarked additions taken from the authentic set of parts where justified for musically obvious reasons (dynamic marks and slurs). The few editorial additions, all warranted by parallel passages, are indicated by parentheses or dotted lines. Further details on source-critical decisions can be found in the tabular overview of alternative readings in the score. The liturgically significant clause "et in unum Dominum Jesum Christum, Filium Dei unigenitum" is not set in the *Credo*; the words "qui ex Patre Filioque procedit" have likewise been omitted.

Klaus Burmeister

---

[1] Many other Masses circulated under Haydn's name, but scholars have long been in agreement that they should be attributed to other composers; see Hob. XXII: C1-B13.

[2] These were the "Kettledrum" Mass (Hob. XXII:9), the "Holy" Mass (no. 10), the "Nelson" Mass (no. 11), the "Theresa" Mass (no. 12), the "Creation" Mass (no. 13) and the "Wind Band" Mass (no. 14).

[3] Haydn's former employer, Prince Nicolaus "the Magnificent", died in 1790. Immediately thereafter his successor, Anton, disbanded the Esterházy orchestra apart from the hunting horns. Following Anton's death on 22 January 1795, however, his successor Nicolaus II re-assembled the orchestra and placed it nominally under Haydn's leadership with the (sole) stipulation that he compose a new Mass each year. Haydn specifically mentions this task in a letter of 10 August 1799 to music director Cornelius Knoblich in Grissau Monastery, remarking that "in his old age" he now had to "compose, at the behest of my then master, the young prince, a new Mass every year for the last four years" (Dénes Bartha, ed.: *Joseph Haydn: Gesammelte Briefe und Aufzeichnungen*, Kassel etc., 1965, p. 331).

[4] It was customary to celebrate the princess's name day (8 September) on the following Sunday, the Feast of the Most Holy Name of Mary.

[5] Peter Rosenbaum wrote "Sunday, the 23rd … at ten o'clock I went to the great church where the new service by Haydn was put on". Translated from Carl Maria Brand, *Die Messen von Joseph Haydn* (Würzburg, 1941), p. 311.

[6] The "Battle of the Nile" near Abukir from 1 to 3 August 1798, in which Admiral Nelson utterly destroyed the French fleet.

[7] "Ueber Musik und Schauspielkunst in Wien", *Journal des Luxus und der Moden*, 15 (Weimar, 1800), pp. 330f. The unknown author heard a performance of the Mass in 1800 in the Schottenkirche in Vienna, and recounted his conversation with Haydn.

[8] Edward Olleson: "Haydn in the Diaries of Count Karl von Zinsendorf", *Haydn-Jahrbuch*, 2 (Vienna, 1963-4), p. 54.

[9] Jens Peter Larsen, ed.: *Drei Haydn Kataloge in Faksimile mit Einleitung und ergänzenden Themenverzeichnissen* (Copenhagen, 1941).

[10] ibid., p. 17.

[11] "Vienna, the 21st of January 1801 …Haydn found a great admirer in Milady Hamilton. She paid a visit with Nelson to Esterházy's estates in Hungary." See Günter Thomas, ed.: "Griesingers Briefe über Haydn", *Haydn-Studien*, i/2 (Munich and Duisburg, 1966), p. 66.

[12] See note 9.

[13] The autograph score lists the following forces on the first page of music: "2 Clarini [although bar 1 of the first Kyrie carries the instruction a tre] / Tympano / Violino 1mo / Violino 2do / Viola / Alto / [vocal parts] Organo [written on two staves]."

[14] Thomas, op. cit., p. 91.

[15] Letter of 15 November 1800, op. cit., p. 66: "Prince Esterházy has enlarged his chapel by eight members so that it once again has a complete wind section."

[16] The handwritten set of parts from the Esterházy Archive has a cover page with the following title: "Anno 1798. / Missa in D. / a / 4. Vocce. Concto. / 2. Violini. / Viola. / Flauto. / 2. Oboi. / 2. Clarinetti / Fagotto. / 2. Corni. / 3. Clarini. / Tympano / Violoncello è Basso. / con. / Organo. / Del Sigre Gius: Haydn." The nickname "Nelson" was added later in a different hand.

[17] The complete title of the first edition in score, issued by Breitkopf & Härtel, reads: "*Messe à 4 Voix avec accompagnement de 2 Violons, Viola et Basse, une Flûte, 2 Hautbois, 2 Bassons, 2 Cors, 3 Trompettes, Timbales et Orgue … No III.*" Oddly, although horns are mentioned in the title, there are none to be found in the print.

[18] Sets of parts with a certain claim to authorial sanction, if only because several copies from the first layer can be attributed to Johann Elssler, are located in Klosterneuburg in Prague (holdings from the Lobkowitz Archive) and Vienna (Archive of the Court Music Chapel). However, none of them contains clarinets or horns, while the Vienna parts, as was the local custom, contain two additional trombones.

[19] *Joseph Haydn Werke*, Ser. XXIII, Vol. 3: *Messen*, nos. 9 and 10 (Munich and Duisburg, 1971).